let every heart

Thomas L. Pless

Illustrations by Don Stewart

PROMISE
PRESS
An Imprint of Barbour Publishing

Contents

FOREWORD

Week Three—Proclamation

God Rest Ye Merry, Gentlemen

Tidings of Comfort and Joy

Tell Out, My Soul, the Greatness

Tell Out the Greatness

I Heard the Bells on Christmas Day

Nor Does He Sleep

Go, Tell It on the Mountain

Go! Tell It!

It Came upon the Midnight Clear

Rest Beside the Weary Road

O Holy Night!

Truly He Taught Us to Love

Break Forth, O Beauteous Heavenly Light

Our Peace Eternal Making

Week Four—Revelation

O Little Town of Bethlehem

How Silently the Wondrous Gift Is Given

Of the Father's Love Begotten

Of the Father's Love

In the Bleak Midwinter

What Can I Give Him?

Angels, from the Realms of Glory

The Infant Light

Good Christian Men, Rejoice

With Heart and Soul and Voice

The Holly and the Ivy

To Be Our Sweet Savior

O Come, All Ye Faithful

Let Us Adore Him!

Christmas Day—Celebration

Joy to the World!

Let Earth Receive Her King

Foreword

Each year, about November first, advertising in America takes on a fiercely competitive demeanor as our holiday dollars are courted by countless commercial entities. Everywhere we turn, it seems, we are faced with an onslaught of entrepreneurial noise. Disembodied voices push "wonderful" new merchandise that neither we nor our children can possibly bear to live without.

As December arrives and the countdown to Christmas continues, we discover that our time is being consumed by countless holiday chores on the one hand, and a host of social obligations on the other. Working, shopping, cooking, cleaning, and entertaining all run together in a blur.

Suddenly, sooner than seems possible, Christmas has come and gone. We find ourselves standing in its wake, reflecting with a strange mixture of satisfaction and disappointment that for better or worse we've survived another holiday season.

Every year we all board a holiday train that picks up such momentum by Thanksgiving that a collision with Christmas is inevitable. Just once, wouldn't you like to slow that train down, stop at a few stations, and enjoy the beauty of the season—instead of just catching glimpses of the holiday's heavenly meaning as it flashes by the windows?

Behold, I bring you tidings of joy! I'm going to share with you a way to slow the pace a bit so that you and your family can enjoy some spiritual fresh air on your holiday journey. Advent is the name of this way. If you are unfamiliar with this special time of year, let me explain that the word "advent" literally means "arrival"; this is a season of preparation for the coming of something—or Someone. It is a time specifically set aside to ready our hearts to receive Christ, the coming King.

This book prompts you to pause and reflect on the Good News: God has given the world a Savior. If you've never experienced a time of worship and spiritual preparation during the Christmas

holidays, enjoy the freshness such an encounter can bring. For those of you already familiar with Advent, let this new approach add life and meaning to an old tradition. Either way, Advent is tailor-made for those of us who hunger for deeper meaning, who are never really satisfied with the mad, materialistic rush so typical of this time of year. Advent helps us recover the missing jewel of Christ's presence during this busy season.

This collection of devotional thoughts is organized around the traditional observance of Advent, which begins on the fourth Sunday before Christmas. The book is designed to help individuals and families recapture a sense of Christmas's deeper significance. Each daily devotional takes as its point of departure a familiar seasonal carol, and each is meant to usher the reader into a time of spiritual reflection and action.

Included here are twenty-nine vignettes, arranged in four seven-day weeks plus Christmas Day. The four groupings conform to the conventional Advent themes of expectation, preparation, proclamation, and revelation. Since the length of Advent changes from year to year, this collection is meant to be flexible. Each selection is freestanding, so the collection can be made to conform to the season's actual length in any given year. (Of course, they can also be used independently of one another to enhance worship services and other gatherings of believers.)

I recommend that you begin your time of worship by singing all the stanzas of each carol or hymn; this will help you prepare your heart for the devotional encounter that follows. Let the familiar words speak anew their timeless message. Then allow the accompanying devotional to guide your thoughts and prayers. Each day's material is followed by several questions for further thought and discussion, and each concludes with a prayer.

Take time daily, either alone or with family or friends, to focus on the coming of the Savior. Christ delights in your attention. Allow Him to speak to your heart, preparing it for the coming celebration of His "arrival."

My hope is that you may truly experience the fullness of this most beautiful time of the year by spending a few joyful moments each day on a spiritual journey. Isaac Watts's famous carol text exclaims, "Let every heart prepare Him room." Let us embrace this thought each day, so that by Christmas Day, our hearts will be ready for our King.

EXPECTATION

The Promise of His Coming

What is a promise? It is a sign of something that is to come. The first week of the Advent season is devoted to reflection on God's faithful promise of a Savior. Through many prophecies, God pledged to His people that a Redeemer would come Who would heal the rift between Earth and heaven. These are words of hope, for great is our spiritual need. In the course of this week we will focus on the tremendous hunger in the soul of human beings apart from God. We will focus, too, on God's faithfulness. He always keeps His promises!

Joy to the World!

Words: Isaac Watts, 1674–1748

Music: George Frederick Handel, 1685–1759
Arr. Lowell Mason, 1792–1872

Let Every Heart Prepare Him Room

The steadfast of mind Thou wilt keep in perfect peace,

because he trusts in Thee.

Isaiah 26:3

The holidays are here! We are standing on the threshold of one of the busiest seasons of the year, a time of shopping and decorating and cooking and entertaining—and we do all of these things on a scale that is truly immense in comparison with our schedule the rest of the year. If we are not careful, the enormous spiritual impact of the season will slip right by without our notice.

As children, my siblings and I made frequent use of a time-honored defense for our misbehavior. When we were caught doing something wrong, we would plead, "But Mom, I didn't mean to!" To which my wise mother would reply, "No, but you didn't mean *not* to." Every year, it seems, we look back on Christmas from the vantage point of the new year and think, "I didn't mean to ignore the spiritual beauty of Christmas in favor of all the temporal trimmings." Well, this year, let's do it differently: Let's mean *not* to. Let's intentionally take time to focus on that beautiful Gift of Life that came to us wrapped in a bundle of swaddling clothes.

Why don't we prepare for Christ's coming this year the way we would prepare for a holiday guest? First, let's clean house. Let's clear out all those sinful, selfish attitudes that would make Him feel less than welcome. Next, let's prepare a meal. Let's make a big buffet of all the things we know He likes, like kindness, humility, and a servant's spirit.

That sounds like a big job, doesn't it? Well, that's what Advent is for. It is a time when we can prepare our hearts to "receive our King." We have an entire month, so if we do a little each day, we should be well and truly ready to entertain the Lord of Glory by Christmas Day.

Let's ask God to help us focus our thoughts on His Son in the coming weeks.

• What positive attitudes can you adopt that will make your heart more fit to "receive your King"?

• What negative attitudes can you make a point to avoid?

• Think of several practical activities that will help you stay in touch with the spiritual side of the holiday. Be creative!

> *Lord, in the rush that will soon be upon us, help us to keep our minds steadfastly stayed on You. After all, You are the reason for our celebration. Guide our words and thoughts as we go about the physical business of Christmas, and bless us with sweet moments in Your presence. Amen.*

What a wonderful picture of the way God grants His peace to us. He does not often still our personal storms, does He? Instead, He tells us to "be still, and know that I am God" (Psalm 46:10, KJV). Then, as we quiet our hearts before Him and allow Him to apply His strength to our troubles, His peace flows into our hearts. It brings order to our inner world, even as life's chaos rages around us.

God is in the business of creating peace where there is only turmoil. Try it and see! Take time right now to "be still" before Him. In the quietness of this moment, make a trade with God: Trade Him your agenda for His agenda. Give Him all your anxieties and fears—and accept His peace in return. Only He can give the inner calm for which you long. He wants you to have it, if you will only take it. Think of it as a Christmas gift from your heavenly Father.

• What are the things that bring stress into your life? Emotionally? Physically? Socially? Spiritually?
• Do you think God will make these stressors disappear if you ask Him? Why or why not?
• Bring your concerns and anxieties to His altar. Offer them by name to the Lord. Ask Him to have His way and to guide you in each of them. Then really let go and let your Father in heaven take over the worrying.

> *In this quiet moment, Lord, I give You all of the fears and stress that trouble my soul. Replace them with a peace that is beyond my comprehension, that I may know that Your hand is at work in my life. Amen.*

Come, Thou Long-Expected Jesus

Words: Charles Wesley, 1707–1788

Music: Rowland H. Prichard, 1811–1887

1. Come, Thou long-ex-pect-ed Je-sus, Born to set Thy peo-ple free;
2. Born Thy peo-ple to de-liv-er, Born a child, and yet a King,

From our fears and sins re-lease us; Let us find our rest in Thee.
Born to reign in us for-ev-er, Now Thy gra-cious king-dom bring.

Is-rael's strength and con-so-la-tion, Hope of all the earth Thou art;
By Thine own e-ter-nal spir-it Rule in all our hearts a-lone;

Dear de-sire of ev-'ry na-tion, Joy of ev-'ry long-ing heart.
By Thine all-suf-fi-cient mer-it, Raise us to Thy glo-rious throne.

Born to Reign in Us

For we are His workmanship, created in Christ Jesus for good works,
which God prepared beforehand, that we should walk in them.

Ephesians 2:10

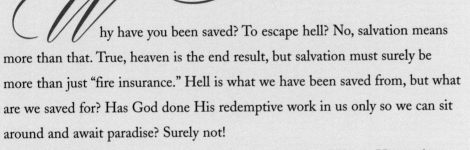

hy have you been saved? To escape hell? No, salvation means more than that. True, heaven is the end result, but salvation must surely be more than just "fire insurance." Hell is what we have been saved from, but what are we saved for? Has God done His redemptive work in us only so we can sit around and await paradise? Surely not!

Ephesians 2:10 provides an answer to our question: "We are His workmanship, created in Christ Jesus for good works." There it is. We are not saved to sit, we are saved to serve! God's plan is for us to accomplish specific works that He has "prepared beforehand." He did His work of redemption in our lives with a concrete goal in mind. We each have a prepared place in His kingdom; He wants us to seek that place, and then to be about the work He has for us. There is no such thing as a holy neutrality. Holiness is active, not passive.

In what is known as the Sermon on the Mount, Jesus made an alarming statement: Not everyone who claims to be subject to His Lordship really is. Instead, He said, you can identify His disciples by what they do (Matthew 7:16–19). The sign of His presence in us is the "fruit" we produce—works that stand out from what we might ordinarily accomplish.

The lyrics of today's carol offer a prayer: "By Thine own eternal spirit, Rule in all our hearts alone."

That surrender of our hearts empowers us to do wonderful things—works of love that require more than just the drive and creativity with which we were born. God's Holy Spirit within our hearts gives us the energy we need; when we allow Him to direct our lives, we are capable of extraordinary things.

In effect, we are saved not only from hell, but also from our own mediocrity. In a very practical way, salvation brings purpose to our lives. We have been set free from the narrow, self-serving existence without Him, emancipated to a meaningful, satisfying life under His rule.

Lordship is not just a metaphor. I believe we are intended to take it seriously. And I believe its natural result is a body of specific works that glorify our Heavenly Father and further His purposes in this world. True, surrender doesn't come easily for us; we're going to need lots of practice. But that is all the more reason to begin immediately! Allow the Lord to search your heart and make known to you those areas you still haven't surrendered to His control. Ask Him to show you the work He has for you to do.

- What signs of Christ's workmanship are evident in your life?
- Are there specific "works" in your life that you are able to accomplish because of God's power working in you? If not, why not?
- Pray this prayer: "Lord, what is Your goal for my life? What do You want to do with me?" He may not answer you immediately, but are you willing to allow Him to make the changes required so that you really are a product of His workmanship?

> *Lord, search my heart and make known to me those things that keep me from Your service. Work in me in such a way so that Your workmanship will be easy to notice. Amen.*

What Child Is This

Words: William C. Dix, 1827–1898

Music: Traditional English Melody, 16th Century
Harm. John Stainer, 1840–1901

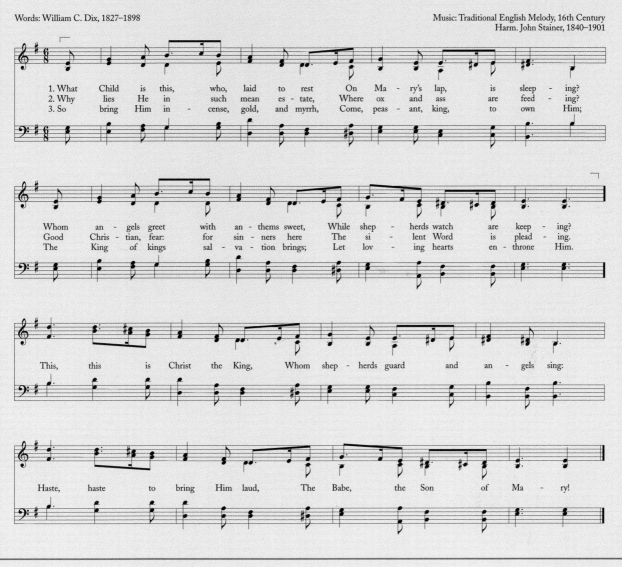

1. What Child is this, who, laid to rest On Mary's lap, is sleep – ing?
2. Why lies He in such mean es – tate, Where ox and ass are feed – ing?
3. So bring Him in – cense, gold, and myrrh, Come, peas – ant, king, to own Him;

Whom an – gels greet with an – thems sweet, While shep – herds watch are keep – ing?
Good Chris – tian, fear: for sin – ners here The si – lent Word is plead – ing.
The King of kings sal – va – tion brings; Let lov – ing hearts en – throne Him.

This, this is Christ the King, Whom shep – herds guard and an – gels sing:

Haste, haste to bring Him laud, The Babe, the Son of Ma – ry!

This Is Christ the King

He said to them, "But who do you say that I am?"

Matthew 16:15

"What Child is this who, laid to rest on Mary's lap, is sleeping?" What Child, indeed? This is perhaps the single most important question any person at any point in history can ask. Who is this Child lying in a manger? Is He really Who Christians claim Him to be? Could He really be the Son of God?

Christian author Josh McDowell, in his book *More Than a Carpenter*,[1] says, "Men and women down through the ages have been divided over the question, 'who is Jesus?' " "Why is it," he goes on to ask, "that His name, more than any other religious leader, causes irritation? Why is it that you can talk about God and nobody gets upset, but as soon as you mention Jesus, people so often want to stop the conversation? . . . The reason is that these others didn't claim to be God, but Jesus did."

You may not have thought about it, but we Christians are not responsible for claiming that Jesus was equal to God. Jesus Himself made these claims. In fact, He said many extraordinary things about Himself. For instance, He said that anyone who had seen Him had seen God the Father (John 14:9). He claimed to have existed before Abraham (John 8:58). He claimed equality with the Father (John 5:17–18). In addition to these and many other such claims about His own nature, Jesus' followers wrote that He created the universe (John 1:3), and that He was actually God in the flesh (1 Timothy 3:16)!

One thing is certain: We cannot write Him off as just another great prophet or teacher. If His claims about Himself are false, then He was at worst a fraud, at best seriously deluded. But if His claims are true, then He is Lord of all creation and deserves our best, most fervent worship and devotion.

"What Child is this?" A lot rides on a person's answer to this question. Every man, woman, boy, and girl must at some point wrestle with it. In the Old Testament, God challenges each of us to "seek Me and find Me" (Jeremiah 29:13). Can He be found in the face of Jesus?

This is not a question you can avoid answering. If you have not yet dealt with this issue, may I encourage you not to sidestep it now? Meet it head-on, honestly asking God's guidance in your search. And commit yourself now to live your life according to the answer you find. God asks no more—but He will accept no less!

- Is Jesus really God in the flesh, as He claimed? Why is this question so important?
- If God, the Creator of the universe, really has presented Himself to us in the flesh, what should our response be? Should it go beyond acts of worship?
- Read Psalm 14:2. What kind of people is God looking for? People who. . .what?
- Are you willing to seek God out? Start with the question, "Christ, who are You? Are You God, or only another prophet? Are You really Lord, or do I just claim that You are?"

> *God, reveal Yourself to me. Guide me as I seek the truth, and use what I find to change my life. Amen.*

Infant Holy, Infant Lowly

Words: Polish Carol
Paraphrased, Edith M.G. Reed, 1885–1933, from Kingsway Carol Book

Music: Polish Carol
Harm. Wilbur Lee

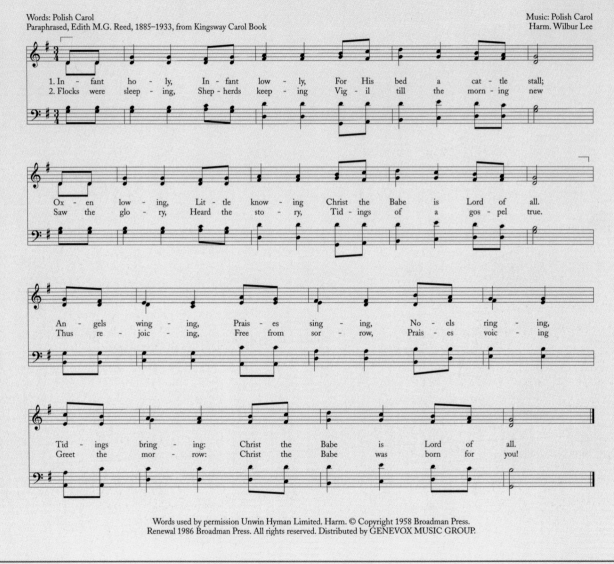

For His Bed a Cattle Stall

The foxes have holes, and the birds of the air have nests;
but the Son of Man has nowhere to lay His head.

Matthew 8:20

What a fascinating juxtaposition of phrases: "Infant holy, Infant lowly." Paired in this way, these two simple descriptions of the Christ Child offer insight into the life we are to lead as Christians.

Often on this world's scale of values, the holy things are relegated to a lowly position. All around us people prize the things that are self-serving, disdaining such "weak" character qualities as gentleness and selflessness. Our society places great emphasis on style, comfort, and ease; but these things have little value. Meanwhile, people ignore and sometimes ridicule the things that have the greatest heavenly significance.

If we are to live as God wants, then we must reconcile ourselves to the fact that we will lead a lowly life. We follow a narrow path that few choose to travel, for holiness and lowliness are constant companions in this world. But we have chosen a life of trial and poverty for a very good reason.

You see, we understand something that many people miss. We know that even though our culture considers holiness a peculiarity, holiness is part of the very order governing the rest of God's creation.

This world, not the righteous folk in it, is actually out of step with reality. In a universe that operates according to divine law and principle, Earth is a lonely outpost of rebellion, exiled from the presence of God, banished from the seat of his holiness.

When Christ came to this world, He entered what must have been to Him a strange place—a place where God's will counts for little. He came to this backward planet to open our blinded eyes, so we could see how far we have wandered from all that is true and good. He had few physical possessions—but then, He came to show us that possessions are not the true measure of success. He did not command great armies—but that is fitting since He taught us that eternal rewards go not to the strong, but to the gentle.

If we follow Christ, then we live as foreigners in this strange land. If we don't speak the language or know the customs, we can be proud that we don't, for we are citizens of a much greater kingdom. As we live these odd, holy lives, God uses our very peculiarities to draw people to Himself. Take heart, believer, and take joy in your uniqueness. God is both living and working in your life.

- What are your personal goals in life?
- What kind of person do you want to be? What personal traits do you admire in others? Who are your heroes?
- What character qualities in your heroes line up with God's values? Which ones don't?
- Are you willing to adjust your life and character in order to be the kind of person God wants you to be?

God, strengthen me to live the life You have called me to. Make my life attractive to the people around me, that they might hunger for You. Amen.

PREPARATION

Following the Light

Just as the magi journeyed from the east, led by a star, so our lives are a journey. We follow the Light of the world, daily seeking to know Him more completely. Thus we are constantly traveling away from the darkness of spiritual death, toward the eternal light of Christlikeness. In this, the second week of Advent, we direct our attention to Christianity's process of enlightenment. We begin now in earnest to prepare our hearts to receive the Prince of Peace.

The First Noel

Words: Traditional English Carol

Traditional English Melody

1. The first No — el, the an — gel did say, Was to cer — tain poor
2. They look — ed up and saw a star Shin — ing in the
3. And by the light of that same star Three wise men
4. This star drew nigh to the north — west, O'er Beth — le —
5. Then en — tered in those wise men three, Full rev — erent —

shep — herds in fields as they lay; In fields where they lay
east, be — yond them far; And to the earth it
came from coun — try far; To seek for a king was
hem it took its rest, And there it did both
ly up — on the knee, And of — fered there, in

keep — ing their sheep, On a cold win — ter's night that was so deep.
gave great light, And so it con — tin — ued both day and night.
their in — tent, And to fol — low the star wher — ev — er it went.
stop and stay, Right o — ver the place where Je — sus lay.
his pres — ence, Their gold and myrrh and frank — in — cense.

Refrain:

No — el, No — el, No — el, No — el, Born is the King of Is — ra — el.

And to the Earth It Gave Great Light

The glory of the Lord has risen upon you.

Isaiah 60:1

"And to the earth it gave great light, and so it continued both day and night." When I read the story of that star that led the wise men to Bethlehem, I must confess to a degree of bewilderment. Standing outside on a cold, clear night, the sky fairly gleams with stars, and they all have one thing in common: They all seem very distant. So I have a hard time picturing how one of these far-off lights could have indicated so precisely where the Christ Child was to be found. We know, though, through Scripture's testimony, that in some way it did occur.

Whatever form that star may have taken, we know it also bore a profound symbolism: The Child in the stable was Himself the One great Light. He came to our dark world to guide our steps. He is the One of whom John said, "There was the true light which, coming into the world, enlightens every man" (John 1:9). He is the One Isaiah foretold when he said to Israel, "The glory of the LORD has risen upon you" (Isaiah 60:1). He is the One who brings light and warmth to our lives, and He is the One who brings the fire of purpose to our souls.

The prophet Isaiah said that, "Nations will come to your light, and kings to the brightness of your rising" (Isaiah 60:3). To better grasp Isaiah's proclamation, imagine an inn built on a hill just off a well-traveled road. On a dark night, its light reaches out like a beacon to every weary traveler, offering rest, nourishment, fellowship, and safety. This is exactly what Christ offers to a tired world. He longs to give rest to our weary hearts and sustenance to our hungry spirits. We are drawn to Him, for He touches something deep in our souls—an empty place we instinctively know only He can fill.

Like that long-ago star, He gives us not only light, but guidance. If you know His warmth and light in your soul, then thank Him for His nurturing care. If you long for the warmth He offers, the Bible says that He is "abounding in riches for all who call upon Him; for 'Whoever will call upon the name of the Lord will be saved' " (Romans 10:12–13). You can call upon Him at any time, even now. Ask Him to come into your life, to save you and fill you. He delights in bringing the light of His love to human hearts.

- Take a good, honest look into your heart. Are there areas of darkness or pain that make you long for warmth, light, and healing? Is there loneliness? Anger? Is there a deep hunger for real love and understanding?
- Christ wants not only to warm those dark, chilly places, but to lead you to a warmer, safer, more fulfilling place. Are you willing to follow Him?
- Pray to Him the prayer below, or one like it. And remember, the road to warmth, light, and safety is not a single step, but a lifelong journey.

> *Lord, come into my heart and fill it with warmth and light. I long for the rest and peace that only You can give. Illumine my soul, guide my steps, and feed my spirit from the stores of Your riches. Be my Sustenance and my Savior. Amen.*

Away in a Manger

Words: St. 1, 2, anonymous, 1885
St. 3, John Thomas McFarland, 1851–1913

Music: James R. Murray, 1841–1905

1. A - way in a man - ger, no crib for a bed, The lit - tle Lord
2. The cat - tle are low - ing, the Ba - by a - wakes, But lit - tle Lord
3. Be near me, Lord Je - sus, I ask Thee to stay Close by me for -

Je - sus laid down His sweet head; The stars in the sky looked
Je - sus, no cry - ing He makes; I love Thee, Lord Je - sus! look
ev - er, and love me, I pray; Bless all the dear chil - dren in

down where He lay, The lit - tle Lord Je - sus a - sleep on the hay.
down from the sky, And stay by my cra - dle till morn - ing is nigh.
Thy ten - der care, And fit us for heav - en to live with Thee there.

And Fit Us for Heaven

He who began a good work in you will perfect
it until the day of Christ Jesus.

Philippians 1:6

What a simple, childlike wonder is expressed in the words of this carol. The unpretentious prayer of faith reminds us what a very special time of year this is for children. Yet this beloved cradle song closes with an eternal truth we grown-ups would do well to remember.

Sometimes, when compiling a collection of songs or hymns, an editor will try to update antiquated words and phrases in order to make them more easily understood by modern singers. We all know that language is not frozen solid; instead it is fluid, continually growing and changing. This is why we have new translations of the Scriptures. All in all, it is not a bad idea to update, or at least to explain, obscure passages.

But the battle for understanding occasionally produces an unfortunate casualty. An example is the very last line of the carol "Away in a Manger," which has at times appeared in print as, "and take us to heaven to live with Thee there." Now stop and think for a moment. That's not exactly what God does with us, is it? He doesn't just take us, no questions asked, and usher us into paradise, does He? Of course not. If we entered heaven in our natural, sinful state, we would spoil that perfect place! No, He must first "fit us for heaven" before He can take us there.

When we receive the Christ of Christmas into our lives to be our Savior, we begin a spiritual journey.

The act of salvation is the starting point of a long and sometimes arduous trek, as God sanctifies us and makes us suitable to dwell in His presence. He uses the joys and the heartaches, the blessings and the trials of everyday life to shape us into Christ's likeness. Like language, the life of a Christian is not frozen solid but is changing and growing. As much as we would like to skip the hard parts, these are some of the very means the Lord employs to smooth off our rough edges and fit us for His kingdom.

Thank God that He cares enough to give you not just what you want, but what you need in order to become like Christ. Like every loving parent, He is more concerned with the outcome of the process than with our momentary discomfort. Today's trouble will be easier to endure when you remember what it is you are being fitted for.

- Can you recall a time in your life when you learned a virtue through a difficult experience? Perhaps you learned patience through a long, difficult circumstance over which you had no control—or trust in God through a serious illness. Describe such a time.
- Could you see at the time that God was building something important into your character? Can you see it clearly now?
- Ask God to make your life more than just a happy time on earth, but a time of growth toward His kingdom.

God, I give You permission to shape my life. Even though I know the process might be painful, I am willing to bear it in order to gain the prize that awaits me. Use whatever means the task requires, that I might accurately portray the image of Your Son. Amen.

As with Gladness Men of Old

Words: William C. Dix, 1837–1898

Music: Conrad Kocher, 1786–1872
Adapt. William Henry Monk, 1823–1889

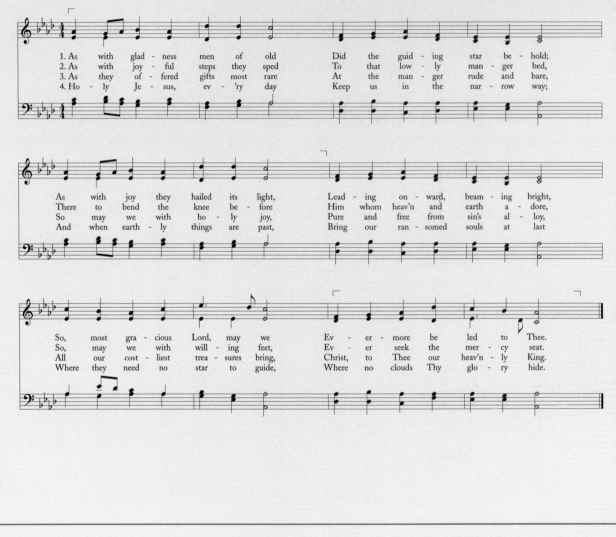

1. As with glad - ness men of old Did the guid - ing star be - hold;
2. As with joy - ful steps they sped To that low - ly man - ger bed,
3. As they of - fered gifts most rare At the man - ger rude and bare,
4. Ho - ly Je - sus, ev - 'ry day Keep us in the nar - row way;

As with joy they hailed its light, Lead - ing on - ward, beam - ing bright,
There to bend the knee be - fore Him whom heav'n and earth a - dore,
So may we with ho - ly joy, Pure and free from sin's al - loy,
And when earth - ly things are past, Bring our ran - somed souls at last

So, most gra - cious Lord, may we Ev - er - more be led to Thee.
So, may we with will - ing feet, Ev - er seek the mer - cy seat.
All our cost - liest trea - sures bring, Christ, to Thee our heav'n - ly King.
Where they need no star to guide, Where no clouds Thy glo - ry hide.

Leading Onward, Beaming Bright

Come. . .and let us walk in the light of the LORD.

Isaiah 2:5

Imagine, if you will, complete, utter darkness, an inky blackness that not even the smallest particle of light can penetrate. Now picture yourself in this absolute void, alone and lost, deprived of your senses, helpless to do anything except wander through an endless maze of obstacles. Now imagine that from above a sharp beam of light miraculously pierces that thick night, shining right where you stand. The light is fixed on you, but it only illuminates your next single step. This is just the way that God's Holy Spirit guides us through the spiritual darkness of our world.

We find rich symbolism in the story of the magi, wise men who traveled to Bethlehem led by the light of a star. Like them, we are being led step-by-step to a place we do not know by a power we do not fully understand.

Another poignant biblical picture of our spiritual journey is the Old Testament account of Israel's sojourn in the wilderness at the time of Moses. We say that the Israelites were "wandering," but that is not strictly true. In fact, they were being led by the visible presence of God, in the form of a "pillar" of cloud by day and a "pillar" of fire by night. Though their journey seemed aimless, God was actually accomplishing an important work in them as He led them from place to place, from event to event. All along that arduous trek He was forging them into a mighty nation, set apart for His glory, through which He would change humanity's eternal destiny. But all along the way they complained, unaware of His greater purpose.

Though our own path sometimes seems aimless, we are never really wandering when we follow God. Though we may not see the big picture—and we may never see it in this life—we can rest assured that there is a big picture. This carol offers the simple prayer: "Holy Jesus, every day keep us in the narrow way." That is exactly how we follow Him: daily. We take a single, trusting step at a time, careful to walk in that beam of light. We do this over and over, day after day. And after many days, led by God's omniscient hand, we too will look up to find ourselves in the promised land, awash in the full light of His glory.

- Can you think of a time when you were required to do something hard, something you didn't want to do, and only later did you see the value of it? As a child, did you ever obey your parents without fully understanding the purpose behind their instructions?
- Has there ever been a time in your walk of faith when God led you through trials? What did He teach you through that experience?
- Things are always clearer in hindsight. But even then, we don't see the big picture. Only God does. Let's give Him free reign to lead us daily in the steps that will lead us home.

Give me faith, Father, to follow where You lead. Teach me to trust in Your plan for me. Though I may not understand the way in which You guide me, give me the faith to follow nonetheless, knowing that I will thank You in the end. Amen.

Let All Mortal Flesh Keep Silence

Words: From the Liturgy of St. James, 5th Century
Tr. Gerard Moultrie, 1829–1885

Music: Traditional French Carol

1. Let all mor-tal flesh keep si-lence, And with fear and trem-bling stand; Pon-der noth-ing earth-ly mind-ed, For with bless-ing in His hand, Christ our God to earth de-scend-eth, Our full hom-age to de-mand.

2. Rank on rank the host of heav-en Spreads its van-guard on the way, As the Light of light de-scend-eth From the realms of end-less day, That the pow'rs of hell may van-ish As the dark-ness clears a-way.

3. At His feet the six-winged ser-aph; Cher-u-bim, with sleep-less eye, Veil their fac-es to the Pres-ence, As with cease-less voice they cry, Al-le-lu-ia! Al-le-lu-ia! Lord Most High.

Ponder Nothing Earthly Minded

Set your minds on the things above, not on the things that are on earth.

Colossians 3:2

What a tremendous gulf exists between heaven and Earth! How great is the expanse between God and humanity. Nothing in this world even approaches the aura of perfection that radiates from the throne of the Almighty. We all fall far short of God's glory. This carol's staid, somber tone compels us to confess a certain discomfort in God's presence. This is the natural response of all that is petty and mundane in our souls to all that is holy and perfect in His.

Isaiah 6:1–8 records that prophet's moving, life-changing experience when he found himself suddenly and unexpectedly standing before the throne of God. His anguished reaction, "Woe is me, for I am ruined!" may not be much like our picture of our first experience of heaven. We like to think of God's kingdom as a paradise where all our tears and pain are banished, where we can cozy up to Christ and ask Him all those questions we have wondered about all our lives. But if we are honest, we must admit that Isaiah's unease resonates all too clearly in our own souls. The Bible tells us that we would never be worthy of heaven without the gift of holiness Christ has placed in our hearts.

Banished as we are to the terrestrial plane, we have a hard time living our lives ever mindful of God's holy presence. We need to cultivate a healthy heavenly-mindedness in our daily walk; we need to practice looking at reality from eternity's perspective. In our own strength we will never attain God's standard of perfection, but we must never forget the power available to us through His Spirit. We have a daily Guide who resides in our hearts, and He can mold our life's clay into a vessel of beauty and strength. On our own we could never create the beautiful shape God has in mind for our vessel—but God can do it.

Do not let your weakness be an excuse for not walking in the Spirit. Knowing that you will fail at times, allow Christ to lend you the power to succeed. Fortunately, God does not ask for perfection; He asks only for submission. Over time, He will do the rest as He shapes you into the image of His Son.

• Do you have what it takes to attain holiness on your own? What does your experience tell you?
• Do you think God is willing to help you become the person He wants you to be?
• What are some of the things that hold us back from wanting to pursue holiness? Discouragement because of past failures? Fear of what we might miss? Others?

> *Spirit of the Living God, fall fresh on me. Break me. Melt me. Mold me.*
> *Fill me. Make me over into the image of Christ, that I may find acceptance*
> *in Your sight. Amen.*

We Three Kings

Words: John Henry Hopkins, Jr., 1820–1891

Music: John Henry Hopkins, Jr., 1820–1891

1. We three kings of Or - i - ent are: Bear - ing gifts we trav - erse a - far—
2. Born a King on Beth - le - hem's plain: Gold I bring to crown Him a - gain,
3. Frank - in - cense to of - fer have I, In - cense owns a De - i - ty nigh;
4. Myrrh is mine, its bit - ter per - fume Breathes a life of gath - er - ing gloom—
5. Glo - rious now be - hold Him a - rise: King and God and Sac - ri - fice;

Field and foun - tain, moor and moun - tain— Fol - low - ing yon - der star.
King for - ev - er, ceas - ing nev - er, O - ver us all to reign.
Prayer and prais - ing, all men rais - ing, Wor - ship Him, God on high.
Sor - r'wing, sigh - ing, bleed - ing, dy - ing, Sealed in the stone - cold tomb.
Al - le - lu - ia, Al - le - lu - ia! Earth to heav'n re - plies.

O star of won - der, star of night, Star with roy - al beau - ty bright,

West - ward lead - ing, still pro - ceed - ing, Guide us to thy per - fect light.

King and God and Sacrifice

And they fell down and worshiped Him; and opening their treasures
they presented to Him gifts of gold and frankincense and myrrh.
Matthew 2:11

This stately hymn recounts the visit of the magi, wise men who journeyed from the east, bearing gifts for the newborn King. It is from them that we derive our tradition of gift-giving at Christmas. The words of this carol illuminate the significance of those first gifts.

"Gold I bring to crown Him. . .King forever." Gold represented Christ's royalty. After all, Christ came to earth to establish a kingdom. His kingdom, though, is not earthly or physical; it is of the spirit. He came to restore our lost race to the realm of God the Father. His kingdom is also personal, for He desires to rule in the heart of every man, woman, boy, and girl. But this regal Conqueror takes no captives. He reigns only in those hearts that willingly surrender to His kingly authority.

Frankincense symbolized Christ's deity. Since ancient times, various cultures have used incense in their worship rites. Its use was a part of the Old Testament temple ritual, representing the prayers and praises of God's people. When the magi gave incense to the Baby, it was a tangible symbol of His divine nature. This was perhaps the first sign that the Messiah was to be not just a righteous servant, but God in human flesh.

Myrrh was used to prepare the bodies of the dead for burial. It was, in fact, one of the spices brought by Nicodemus to anoint Jesus' body after His death. Its presentation at the nativity foreshadows "a life of gathering gloom," and reminds us that Christ came to die, paying the penalty for humanity's sins.

At Christmastime we celebrate God's gift to us: His Son, Who was at once King and God and Sacrifice. As our King, we crown Him once again, reaffirming His right to reign on the individual thrones of our lives. As our God, we bow before Him with a sense of awe at His greatness and worth. And we humbly accept His sacrifice, a gift of indescribable worth. In return, we can make Christmas an opportunity to give Him the gift He treasures most: our hearts.

• What is the greatest gift God has given you?

• What is the greatest gift you can give to God? Is it some religious act or great work of compassion? Is it the sacrifice of something you love? Or is it even deeper than that?

> *Christ Jesus, I crown You King of my life and reaffirm Your right to rule in my heart. I recognize You as my God, worthy of the best of my worship. With a humble heart I accept the gift of Your sacrifice for my sin. Take my heart as my gift to You. Amen.*

Gentle Mary Laid Her Child

Words: Joseph Simpson Cook, 1859–1933

Music: A Spring Carol, c. 14th Century
Arr. Ernest MacMillan, 1893–1973

1. Gen - tle Ma - ry laid her Child Low - ly in a man - ger;
2. An - gels sang a - bout His birth; Wise men sought and found Him;
3. Gen - tle Ma - ry laid her Child Low - ly in a man - ger;

There He lay, the un - de - filed, To the world a stran - ger:
Heav - en's star shone bright - ly forth, Glo - ry all a - round Him:
He is still the un - de - filed, But no more a stran - ger:

Such a Babe in such a place, Can He be the Sav - ior?
Shep - herds saw the won - drous sight, Heard the an - gels sing - ing;
Son of God, of hum - ble birth, Beau - ti - ful the sto - ry;

Ask the saved of all the race, Who have found His fa - vor.
All the plains were lit that night, All the hills were ring - ing.
Praise His name in all the earth, Hail the King of glo - ry!

Can He Be the Savior?

So then, you will know them by their fruits.

Matthew 7:20

During the Easter season, and at other times of the year, we sing a song that proclaims, "you ask me how I know He lives; He lives within my heart." The same truth—that Christ gives us internal evidence of His presence—is echoed in the lines of this carol: "Such a Babe in such a place, can He be the Savior? Ask the saved of all the race who have found His favor."

One thing that makes Christianity unique among the world's religions is that we follow not a teacher but a savior. The teaching of Jesus Christ is not central to our faith; Jesus Christ Himself is. No amount of training or philosophizing can change the fundamental flaw of original sin in each of us.

Only the presence of the dynamic person of Christ can work that change.

Scripture teaches that the Lord's entrance into the human heart is not just a spiritual event. Instead, it is a tangible happening that brings its own concrete evidence. God's Spirit produces in us such fruit as "love, joy, peace, patience, kindness, goodness, faithfulness, gentleness, [and] self-control" (Galatians 5:22–23). The unregenerate human heart would never be able to produce these qualities so abundantly.

Christmas is a good time to examine what the Bible calls our "inner man" for signs of His presence. Using the list from

Galatians as a guide, inspect your "spiritual orchard," testing the quality of each type of fruit being produced there. If you find an abundance, don't gloat! But if, like most of us, you find certain qualities lacking, use these as clues to areas in your life that need to be surrendered to Christ's care.

If you have yet to experience His presence in your life, you may ask Him right now to be your Savior. Let Him do that work in your life that only He can do.

- Which crop of fruit mentioned in Galatians 5:22–23 do you find most in abundance in your life?
- Which of the fruit is most lacking? Be honest!
- Do you believe that Christ can produce these things in your heart where you have been unable to produce them yourself? Take a risk and ask Him to do just that. Then see what He does!

> *Lord, examine my heart and change anything there that You find displeasing. Produce Your healthy fruit in me. Build in me all those qualities I want to have but cannot produce in myself. Amen.*

Thou Didst Leave Thy Throne

Words: Emily E.S. Elliott, 1836–1897

Music: Timothy R. Matthews, 1826–1910

1. Thou didst leave Thy throne and Thy king - ly crown, When Thou
2. Heav - en's arch - es rang when the an - gels sang, Pro -
3. The fox - es found rest, and the birds their nest In the
4. Thou cam - est, O Lord, with the liv - ing word That should
5. When the heav - ens shall ring, and the an - gels sing, At Thy

cam - est to earth for me; But in Beth - le - hem's home was there
claim - ing Thy roy - al de - gree; But of low - ly birth didst Thou
shade of the for - est tree; But Thy couch was the sod, O Thou
set Thy peo - ple free; But with mock - ing scorn, and with
com - ing to vic - to - ry, Let Thy voice call me home say - ing

found no room For Thy ho - ly na - tiv - i - ty.
come to earth, And in great hu - mil - i - ty.
Son of God, In the des - erts of Gal - i - lee.
crown of thorn, They bore Thee to Cal - va - ry.
"Yet there is room, There is room at My side for thee."

1–4. O come to my heart, Lord Je - sus, There is room in my heart for Thee.
5. My heart shall re - joice, Lord Je - sus, When Thou com - est and call - est for me.

52

There Is Room in My Heart

If any one hears My voice and opens the door, I will come in to him.

Revelation 3:20

"Although He existed in the form of God, [He] did not regard equality with God a thing to be grasped, but. . .being found in appearance as a man, He humbled Himself" (Philippians 2:6–8). Ironically, while heaven's arches rang with the sound of the angels' praises, the holy Baby slept in a rough feeding trough in a barn. In the earthly realm, unlike the heavenly, other matters superseded Him in importance; there were fortunes to be made, advantages to be seized, other, more "influential" people to be pleased. No one was expecting a miracle that night. Wouldn't there, after all, be some kind of notice prior to the arrival of One so great? So momentous an event in history would rate some advanced publicity, surely! But no, then as now, Christ preferred the soft sell. There, amid the babble of commercial and domestic life, lay the King of Glory, patiently awaiting the world's notice. Ever the Gentleman, He still waits for humans to make room for Him in their lives.

Revelation 3:20 gives us an interesting picture of Jesus' unique "sales technique," the means by which He attempts to gain access to our hearts. In this passage Christ says, "Behold, I stand at the door and knock; if any one hears My voice and opens the door, I will come in to him. . . ." Think about it: "if any one hears My voice." If we are to have fellowship with Him, we must first hear His voice. Somehow we must break free of the tyranny of those thousand little urgencies that compete for our attention. If we are to avoid repeating the mistake of the hundreds of people packing Bethlehem's inns that night, we must intentionally make time to listen for His voice. It comes only softly through the cacophony of our everyday world.

"O come to my heart, Lord Jesus; there is room in my heart for Thee." Couldn't this be our holiday theme? Let's ask God to work supernaturally in our lives to help us keep first things first. We need to prioritize the long list of "to-dos" in our minds in such a way that we have time for Him.

- Everyone has an agenda. What is yours? What is your agenda for this week? What is on your lifelong agenda?
- What is the loudest, most demanding thing on your agenda? This week? This year?
- Nothing is worth crowding out Christ's still small voice from your daily existence. How can you rearrange some of those urgent matters, those seemingly crucial items on your list, so that you can make room for Him and listen for His voice?

> *Come to my heart, Lord Jesus. Be at home there. Rearrange things to suit Your tastes, if need be, but come to my heart. There is room in my heart for You. Amen.*

PROCLAMATION

Tidings of Great Joy

The angels proclaimed to the shepherds the news of a great joy that was for all people—those who were alive then, all who were born and lived through the intervening years, up to and including the people of our generation. This week, the third in the season of Advent, we will concentrate on the magnitude of that message and its implications today—both for our own lives and for the lives of those who inhabit our personal world.

God Rest Ye Merry, Gentlemen

Words: Traditional English Carol, 18th Century

Music: Traditional English Melody

1. God rest ye mer - ry, gen - tle - men, Let noth - ing you dis - may,
2. In Beth - le - hem in Is - ra - el This bless - ed babe was born,
3. From God our heaven - ly Fa - ther A bless - ed an - gel came,
4. The shep - herds at those tid - ings Re - joic - ed much in mind,
5. Now to the Lord sing prais - es, All you with - in this place,

For Je - sus Christ our Sav - ior Was born up - on this day,
And laid with - in a man - ger Up - on this bless - ed morn:
And un - to cer - tain shep - herds Brought tid - ings of the same,
And left their flocks a - feed - ing In tem - pest, storm, and wind,
And with true love and broth - er - hood Each oth - er now em - brace;

To save us all from Sa - tan's power When we were gone a - stray.
The which his moth - er Ma - ry Did noth - ing take in scorn.
How that in Beth - le - hem was born The Son of God by name.
And went to Beth - le - hem straight - way, The bless - ed babe to find.
This ho - ly tide of Christ - mas All oth - er doth de - face.

Refrain:

O tid - ings of com - fort and joy, com-fort and joy; O tid - ings of com - fort and joy!

Tidings of Comfort and Joy

Let the peace of Christ rule in your hearts.

Colossians 3:15

ere's a riddle: Did you know that this carol has nothing whatsoever to do with wise men? It's true! Look carefully at the stanzas. Regardless of its usage in all the Christmas pageants you have seen, you will see that the words tell not of the magi resting at the end of their long journey, but of the shepherds and their journey to Bethlehem to see the Baby in the manger. But wait! There is more to the mystery, for the shepherds are not the "gentlemen" the carol has in mind either. Who are those gentlemen we have been singing about all these years? Have you guessed it yet? "Gentlemen" refers to. . .us!

"God rest ye merry" is an Old English way of saying, "God give you peace" or, "God keep you merry." It is a wish that nothing would dismay or disturb the one receiving the blessing, but that he or she would be happy and content. Today we might say, "God's peace be yours." In this song the blessing refers not to a physical rest, but to a holy relaxation of the soul made possible because "Jesus Christ our Savior was born. . .to save us all from Satan's power." The "tidings of comfort and joy" is the message that Christ's redemptive work on the cross has made us no longer at odds with our Creator but at peace. This is the same good news that Luke tells us "shall be to all people": God has sent a Redeemer to restore us to His presence.

In this season of celebration, relax in that special sense of completeness that God gives the redeemed. As you sing the songs of Christmas and read the timeless story of Christ's birth, exult in the joy that comes from knowing you have received the best Christmas gift of all: the right to stand in God's presence, a member of His royal family, secure for eternity.

• Have you ever known someone who seemed full of both joy and peace at the same time? What do you think is that person's secret?

• "Resting merry" means being at peace, yet full of joy. Where do you think such peace comes from? Such joy?

• What distractions or complications tend to rob you of the simplicity of living in the light of Christ's joy and peace?

> *Lord, thank You for redeeming me from a state of sin and setting me securely at Your side. No other gift could be half so precious. My heart is glad and my soul rejoices in You. Amen.*

Tell Out, My Soul, the Greatness

Words: Timothy Dudley-Smith, 1926–

Music: Walter Greatorex, 1877–1949

1. Tell out, my soul, the great-ness of the Lord: Un-num-bered bless-ings give my spir-it voice; Ten-der to me the prom-ise of His word; In God my Sav-ior shall my heart re-joice.

2. Tell out, my soul, the great-ness of His name: Make known His might, the deeds His arm has done; His mer-cy sure, from age to age the same; His ho-ly name, the Lord, the Might-y One.

3. Tell out, my soul, the great-ness of His might: Powr's and do-min-ions lay their glo-ry by; Proud hearts and stub-born wills are put to flight, The hun-gry fed, the hum-ble lift-ed high.

4. Tell out, my soul, the glo-ries of His word: Firm is His prom-ise, and His mer-cy sure. Tell out, my soul, the great-ness of the Lord To chil-dren's chil-dren and for-ev-er-more.

Tell Out the Greatness

For the Mighty One has done great things for me.

Luke 1:49

"We're Marching to Zion," a grand old song of the Christian "army," has for many years been an encouragement to believers who are doing Christ's work. One rather enigmatic line of the song says, "let those refuse to sing who never knew our God; but children of the heavenly King may speak their joys abroad." This is not saying, of course, that unbelievers can't sing. It simply means that those who have never known Christ might well have nothing to sing about—but His children just can't help themselves! Whenever I get to that part of the song, I am always reminded of Simeon. You know, Simeon. At the temple. No? Well, let me tell you about him.

Luke 2:25–35 records that Simeon was a righteous man to whom it had been revealed by the Holy Spirit that he would "not see death before he had seen the Lord's Christ." On the day Jesus' parents brought Him to the temple to fulfill the requirements of Moses' law, Simeon was also "driven" by the Spirit to the temple. When he saw the Child, Simeon began to bless God and prophesy. That sounds rather dry, but believe me, Simeon was excited! He was experiencing the greatest event of his long life, one for which he had fervently sought the Lord for many years. Now, before his very eyes, God's promise was revealed. Simeon couldn't have refused to broadcast the good news even if he had wanted to; he was too overwhelmed with the greatness of God's message.

Have you ever been so excited about something that you just had to share it, if only with a perfect stranger? I was that way when our babies were born. I imagine that many a passerby came to regret their courteous "how do you do?" For them it was just another ordinary day; for me it was the event of a lifetime. That is the way I picture Simeon that day, telling everyone in his path that the Messiah was born, whether or not they wanted to hear it. His joy just bubbled over until it had to spill out onto the world around him. Oh, what some of us wouldn't give to experience that kind of joy.

Obviously, we cannot expect that level of excitement on a daily basis. But the Bible does tell us that joy is a part of the fruit of Christ's presence in our lives. What does that mean? It means simply that joy is a by-product of our relationship with Him. It is not available in the same measure to the general public. It is not available to those who only know about Him. It may not even be evident in the hearts of those who are trying to serve Him. It is reserved for those who actually know Him. Real joy is not the product of what we know or do. Real joy emanates from the person of Christ and comes to those who regularly fellowship with Him. Would you like to know joy? Then get to know Christ, for it is in His presence that we find true joy.

- Look back at the words of this carol. It speaks of "unnumbered blessings." What are some of the blessings He has granted you?
- Name some of the "deeds His arm has done" in your life.
- How has He shown His "firm promise" and "sure mercy" to you?
- All these are evidences of His presence in and around you. Don't take them for granted. Rather, consider them His way of introducing Himself to you. Reach out and begin to know not just Christ's deeds, but Christ Himself.

Lord, help me to know You, and not just know about You. You have promised that those who seek You will find You, so show me where to begin. Guide me into Your presence, for I know I will never be satisfied with anything less. Amen.

I Heard the Bells on Christmas Day

Words: Henry W. Longfellow, 1807–1882

Music: John Calkin, 1827–1905

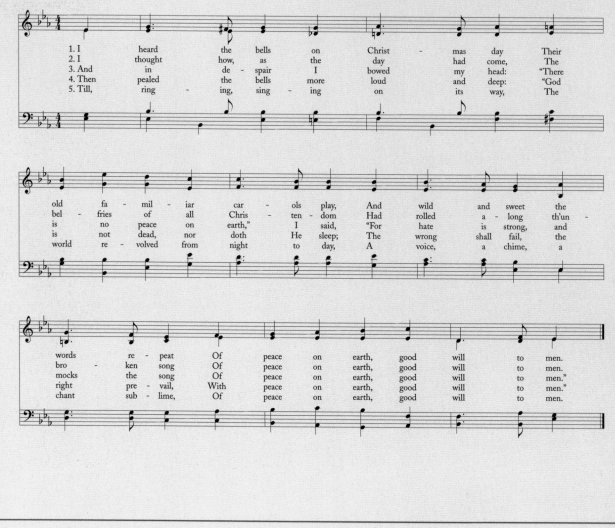

1. I heard the bells on Christ - mas day Their
2. I thought how, as the day had come, The
3. And in de - spair I bowed my head: "There
4. Then pealed the bells more loud and deep: "God
5. Till, ring - ing, sing - ing on its way, The

old fa - mil - iar car - ols play, And wild and sweet the
bel - fries of all Chris - ten - dom Had rolled a - long th'un -
is no peace on earth," I said, "For hate is strong, and
is not dead, nor doth He sleep; The wrong shall fail, the
world re - volved from night to day, A voice, a chime, a

words re - peat Of peace on earth, good will to men.
bro - ken song Of peace on earth, good will to men.
mocks the song Of peace on earth, good will to men."
right pre - vail, With peace on earth, good will to men."
chant sub - lime, Of peace on earth, good will to men.

Nor Doth He Sleep

The Son of Man has come to seek and to save that which was lost.

Luke 19:10

The year is 1864. America's bloody Civil War is raging. And it is Christmas. A season set aside, supposedly, to celebrate peace and brotherly love, thinks poet Henry Wadsworth Longfellow as he ponders headlines full of carnage and destruction. Surveying the sad scenes played out in the world around him, Longfellow observes that "hate is strong, and mocks the song of peace on earth, good will to men."

Things have not changed much in the intervening years, have they? Today the headlines are still harbingers of bad news: civil war, ethnic violence, child abuse, savage acts of crime. All these seem to flourish now more than ever before. How do we reconcile Christ's having come into the world with the existence of so much misery and evil? Looking around us, we see scant evidence of His presence. Where is the peace and love He was supposed to bring? In the face of so much wrong, how can we honestly claim that Jesus is Lord?

This sad state of affairs is exactly why Christ came into the world. Without Him, we have no hope of ever achieving lasting peace on earth. Why? Because we humans are naturally selfish. Without His presence in our hearts, we have not the capacity for sustained, selfless love, and without love we are incapable of the kind of mutual respect that breeds peace. You see, Jesus did not come simply to banish the symptoms of sin. He came to treat the cause of sin, the self-centered nature of humanity. He came to work a fundamental change in each person's heart, changing the world one person at a time. The wrong that we see around us is only a vivid reminder that He has not yet been made welcome in every heart.

What can we do to make a real difference in our world? First, we can determine to let Him rule in our own hearts completely. Then we can earnestly pray, and act, so that others will come to know Him as their Savior and Lord. God wants to change the evil that is rampant in the world around us. Our hesitancy to let Him begin in us is the only thing that limits Him.

• What evidences of evil and hate do you see in the world around you?

• Do you think God would like to change these things? Why doesn't He?

• Closer to home, what evidences of selfishness do you see in your own life? Think hard, and be honest.

• Do you think God wants to change these areas in your life? How can He do that?

> *Lord, begin changing my world by first changing me. Take complete control of my heart. Then, through me, touch those around me, and let the world know the peace and goodness that come from Your hand. Amen.*

Go, Tell It on the Mountain

Words: John W. Work, Jr., 1872–1925

Music: Negro spiritual
Harm. John W. Work, III, 1901–1967

Go, tell it on the moun - tain, O - ver the hills and ev - 'ry - where;

Go, tell it on the moun - tain That Je - sus Christ is born!

1. While shep - herds kept their watch - ing O'er si - lent flocks by night,
2. The shep - herds feared and trem - bled When lo! a - bove the earth
3. Down in a low - ly man - ger The hum - ble Christ was born,

Be - hold thro' - out the heav - ens There shone a ho - ly light.
Rang out the an - gel cho - rus That hailed our Sav - ior's birth.
And God sent us sal - va - tion That bless - ed Christ - mas morn.

Harmonization used by permission, Mrs. John W. Work, III.

Go! Tell It!

And all who heard it wondered at the things which
were told them by the shepherds.

Luke 2:18

In our culture they would have worn blue collars. The shepherds were the working class of their day. They had probably done nothing to merit an angelic visit; they were just ordinary men doing an ordinary job on an ordinary night. So when an angel of the Lord suddenly appeared, and the glory of the Lord illuminated the countryside, they were overwhelmed!

The shepherds' reaction to the angels' visit was to tell everyone they met what they had seen and heard. Now, it would be all too tempting to oversimplify the modern-day moral of their story, by saying that we, too, should be going and telling. But that is not the real lesson to be learned from the shepherds. Rather, the lesson is this: We cannot expect to be motivated to go and tell unless we have something to tell. What we should learn from these men of old is to keep our experience with the Lord up-to-date. After all, people don't want to hear our old news; and, let's face it, neither do we relish telling it. But if we can learn to tell the world not what God has done for us, but what He is doing, we will be the bearers of good news indeed.

The shepherds' response was the natural one, given the amazing event they had just witnessed. Their news made people marvel and wonder. Do we have news that wondrous? One young pastor I know coined a word to describe the people in our culture: "gospel-logged." That is, they have been so exposed to copious amounts of religion, so saturated with it, that they hardly take notice anymore. So no one is standing in line to hear about our theology. People are bored with hearing the same old, out-of-date news.

But these very same people are longing to know that there is a personal Savior who loves them deeply. The best way for them to see Him is through His current, daily activity in the lives of those who already know Him. Is there evidence of His daily activity in your life? Is He doing wondrous things for you? If not, it is through no lack of willingness on His part.

- What do you have to tell? If someone stopped you on the street and asked about your relationship with Christ, what would you say?
- Examine your response. Were you relating "old news" from the distant past? Did your words seem watered-down, full of theological truth but little excitement? Did you find yourself describing a few isolated personal encounters?
- Would you like to know Christ in a very real way on a current, ongoing basis? He waits to engage you in just such a relationship. Ask Him to make your heart sensitive to His voice and His presence.

> *Lord, set me free from boring religion. Talking about what You have done in the past is no longer good enough for me. I want to see You in action in my life. Remove whatever obstacles are keeping You from making Yourself known through me. Amen.*

It Came upon the Midnight Clear

Words: Edmund H. Sears, 1810–1876

Music: Richard Storrs Willis, 1819–1900

1. It came up-on the mid - night clear, That glo - rious song of old,
2. Yet with the woes of sin and strife The world has suf - fered long,
3. All ye, be - neath life's crush - ing load, Whose forms are bend - ing low,
4. For lo! the days are has - t'ning on, By proph - et bards fore - told,

From an - gels bend - ing near the earth, To touch their harps of gold:
Be - neath the an - gel strain have rolled Two thou - sand years of wrong;
Who toil a - long the climb - ing way With pain - ful steps and slow,
When with the ev - er - cir - cling years Comes round the age of gold;

"Peace on the earth, good will to men," From heav'n's all - gra - cious King.
And man, at war with man, hears not The love song which they bring;
Look now! for glad and gold - en hours Come swift - ly on the wing:
When peace shall o - ver all the earth Its an - cient splen - dors fling,

The world in sol - emn still - ness lay, To hear the an - gels sing.
O hush the noise, ye men of strife, And hear the an - gels sing!
O rest be - side the wea - ry road, And hear the an - gels sing!
And the whole world give back the song Which now the an - gels sing.

70

Rest Beside the Weary Road

Come to Me, all who are weary. . .and I will give you rest.

Matthew 11:28

An old familiar gospel song asks the question, "Are you weary, are you heavy-laden?" then goes on to counsel, "tell it to Jesus." A similar sense of heaviness is captured in the words of this carol, directed to those of us who sometimes feel the full weight of life's crushing load, whose "forms are bending low" beneath an overwhelming burden of care.

Somewhere in young adulthood, the blind optimism of our youth fades as it comes into conflict with the realities of this sometimes harsh and difficult world. It is the wise, well-balanced person who can accept life's problems for what they are, no more and no less, deal with them, and get on with the excitement of living. Unfortunately, all too often those obstacles can send us into a tailspin from which it is difficult to recover.

Have hope! There is good news for the heavy-laden. We have a merciful Savior who cares for us deeply. The Scriptures assure us again and again that He loves us, not just in some universal sense, but with a personal love that takes our daily needs into account. You see, Christ has reconciled us to God, and in doing so has opened the door to the very dwelling place of the Most High. He will help shoulder our heavy load.

Rest assured, weary one. God has invited us to lay all our anxieties upon His shoulder (1 Peter 5:7). He also promises that if we will acknowledge Him in all our ways, He will give direction to our paths (Proverbs 3:6). Maybe you have never taken the opportunity to commit the events of your life to Him. Perhaps you would like to do so now. If you think about it, in what better hands could you be?

Take a quiet moment to commit or recommit your life to the One Who cares most about you. Roll upon His broad shoulders the cares and burdens of your existence. Allow Christ to do the heavy work for awhile, while you relax in His loving care.

- What burdens weigh you down? What irritations wear away at you? What makes your soul tired?
- Would you be open to some heavenly help? Read 1 Peter 5:7.
- Now name your burdens to Him. Loosen your grip and one by one transfer them into His care. Let Him carry them and guide you through them. Relax in His peace as you trust Him to be at work in these areas of your life.

Father, take the burdens and irritations that have been wearing me down, and put in their place Your peace. I commit myself to You now. Help me to be a trusting servant while You work Your will in me. Amen.

O Holy Night!

Words: John S. Dwight

Music: Adolphe Adam

yon - der breaks a new and glo - rious morn. Fall on your knees. Oh,
all our tri - als born to be our Friend. He knows our need; our To
all with - in us praise His ho - ly name; Christ is the Lord, Oh,

hear the an - gel voic - es! O night di -
weak - ness is no stran - ger. Be - hold
praise His name for - ev - er! His pow'r and

vine, O night when Christ was born! O
your King, be - fore Him low - ly bend! His
glo - - - ry ev - er - more pro - claim! His

Cued notes opt. on last refrain

night, O ho - ly night, O night di - vine!
Be - hold your King, be - fore Him low - ly
pow'r and glo - ry ev - er - more pro - claim.

75

Truly He Taught Us to Love

To the extent that you did it to one of these brothers of Mine,
even the least of them, you did it to Me.
Matthew 25:40

Have you ever heard anyone say that someone is "so heavenly minded he's no earthly good"? In reality, if our minds are truly focused on heaven, we cannot help but be of great good here on Earth. Even so, we Christians are sometimes guilty of narrow-mindedness, concerning ourselves exclusively with spiritual matters while we ignore the gospel's potential impact on other aspects of human existence.

Feeding, educating, and protecting the citizens of the world is not our first priority as Christians. Were we to concentrate solely on meeting these external needs, we would be missing the very essence of the gospel's message, namely that humanity is in desperate need of an internal, spiritual change. But neither can we live in a spiritual vacuum; by giving attention only to matters of the heart, we may be missing much of the meat of our faith. James 2:17 warns us that "faith, if it has no works, is dead." Not sick, not ineffective. Dead. It might as well not exist at all.

What are our society's needs? Hunger? Poverty? Lack of education? Yes, these are all areas of need, but look closer. What about loneliness? Instability in the family? Lack of purpose? The suicide rate? The fact that so many of these needs are not met as a by-product of our faith suggests that we may be "more hearers than doers of the word." As Rebecca Manley Pippert[2] so aptly put it in the title of her book, we need to get "out of the salt shaker and into the world." When we leave our sanctuaries each week, we must be willing to be the salt of the earth and the light of the world. If we keep our faith private, then we really are of no earthly good.

Christ did not separate humanity's spiritual condition from the resulting physical symptoms. He came, He said, "to preach the gospel to the poor. . .to proclaim release to the captives, and recovery of sight to the blind, to set free those who are downtrodden" (Luke 4:18). He knew that by concerning Himself with people's tangible problems, He would earn the right to address the need of their souls for salvation. In passing on that commission to us, He must surely expect no less an effort, no smaller love. By demonstrating Christ's love we will make the world hungry for His presence in their hearts.

- Can you think of someone you know who is in need this season? A lonely neighbor? A young man stationed far from home? Someone who has been through recent pain or crisis?
- What can you do for that person this season to demonstrate Christ's love and care? How can you show Christ's heart through your gift?
- What are some things you can do year-round to show Christ's love to people around you? Think of some simple things. Now think of some projects that involve a greater commitment of time, energy, and love.

Lord, stretch my faith beyond the confines of my heart. Let me know the joy of showing Your love to the people in my world. Make me to shine in the darkness around me, that the lost may see You and long to know You. Amen.

Break Forth, O Beauteous Heavenly Light

Words: St.1, Johann Rist, 1607–1667
St. 2, A.T. Russell, 1806–1874

Music: Johann Schop, c. 1590–1664
Harm. Johann Sebastian Bach, 1685–1750

1. Break forth, O beau-teous heav'n-ly light, And ush-er in the morn-ing; O
2. Break forth, O beau-teous heav'n-ly light, To her-ald our sal-va-tion; He

shep-herds, shrink not with af-fright, But hear the an-gel's warn-ing. This
stoops to earth— the God of might, Our hope and ex-pec-ta-tion. He

Child, now weak in in-fan-cy, Our con-fi-dence and joy shall be, The
comes in hu-man flesh to dwell, Our God with us, Im-man-u-el, The

pow'r of Sa-tan break-ing, Our peace e-ter-nal mak-ing.
night of dark-ness end-ing, Our fall-en race be-friend-ing.

Our Peace Eternal Making

For if by the transgression of one, death reigned through the one,
much more those who receive the abundance of grace. . .will reign in life
through the One, Jesus Christ.

Romans 5:17

Just before Adam and Eve were banished from the garden of Eden, God made a rather mysterious promise to the serpent: In Genesis 3:15 He told the serpent that the woman's offspring would ". . . bruise you on the head." We understand this today, of course, to be the prophecy of Satan's defeat at the hands of a son of man, the Savior Jesus Christ.

In 1 Corinthians 15:21–22, the apostle Paul speaks of Christ as a kind of second Adam when he says, "For since by a man came death, by a man also came the resurrection of the dead. For as in Adam all die, so also in Christ all shall be made alive." This is a striking word picture, for Christ was indeed our second chance at eternity. He represented, in effect, our return engagement on the battlefield of Eden. He became our victory. This stately German chorale captures the essence of this victorious side of Christmas with these words:

This Child, now weak in infancy,

Our confidence and joy shall be,

The pow'r of Satan breaking,

Our peace eternal making.

What a wonderfully succinct reminder that God took on human form and, as one of our own, won back our right to eternal life.

A famous hymn penned by Charles Wesley says, "He breaks the power of canceled sin; He sets the prisoner free." Think about these words: Through Christ, the power of sin is canceled, negated, done away with. In our minds we know this is true on a universal scale—but does it also have bearing on the way we live our daily lives?

Studying the New Testament, we find over and over the admonition to be holy. Yet our experience seems to demonstrate that sinlessness is always just beyond our reach. What a quandary! The answer to this dilemma is this: We cannot be perfect, but we can be holy, set apart for God. By allowing Him access to the world of our daily thoughts and actions, we can know the benefit of His Spirit's power at work in our lives, making us daily more and more like Christ.

Take time right now to recommit your daily life to Him. In doing so, you will open yourself to a whole new realm of spiritual activity. This lively spirituality reaches far beyond the limits of mere theology.

- 1 John 1:9 reminds us to confess our sins to the Lord. Spend a few moments quietly before the Lord. Use this time to examine your heart and ask His forgiveness for specific sins.
- Now read 1 John 1:9. Do you see His promise of forgiveness?
- There is a second promise in this verse. What is it?
- Read Philippians 1:6. What connection do you see between God's promise of cleansing and this verse? Is His cleansing a one-time thing, or is it an ongoing process?

> *Lord, let me know by experience what Your victory over sin means. I invite You to be an active part of my life, today and in the coming days. Accomplish in me, day by day, Your ultimate work, that I might know what it is to have victory. Amen.*

REVELATION

Love's Greatest Gift

The fourth week of Advent is set aside to consider God's wondrous, awesome gift to us: the gift of His Son Jesus Christ. God longs so much to dwell with us that He would die for the chance. How incredible is the depth of His love! In these final days in the countdown to Christmas, we meditate on that gift of love revealed, as we contemplate its potential impact upon our lives.

O Little Town of Bethlehem

"Out of you will come ... one who will be ruler over Israel" — Micah 5:2 NIV

Words: Phillips Brooks, 1835–1893

Music: Lewis H. Redner, 1831–1908

1. O lit - tle town of Beth - le - hem, How still we see thee lie!
2. For Christ is born of Ma - ry, And gath - ered all a - bove,
3. How si - lent - ly, how si - lent - ly The won - drous gift is giv'n!
4. O ho - ly Child of Beth - le - hem! De - scend to us, we pray;

A - bove thy deep and dream - less sleep The si - lent stars go by;
While mor - tals sleep, the an - gels keep Their watch of won - d'ring love.
So God im - parts to hu - man hearts The bless - ings of His heav'n.
Cast out our sin, and en - ter in, Be born in us to - day!

Yet in thy dark streets shin - eth The ev - er - last - ing Light;
O morn - ing stars, to - geth - er Pro - claim the ho - ly birth,
No ear may hear His com - ing, But in this world of sin,
We hear the Christ - mas an - gels The great glad tid - ings tell;

The hopes and fears of all the years Are met in thee to - night.
And prais - es sing to God the King, And peace to men on earth!
Where meek souls will re - ceive Him, still The dear Christ en - ters in.
O come to us, a - bide with us, Our Lord Im - man - u - el!

How Silently the Wondrous Gift Is Given

In quietness and trust is your strength.
Isaiah 30:15

"How silently the wondrous gift is given. So God imparts to human hearts the blessings of His heaven." Without fanfare, to no applause, Christ was born into the world. Our worldly minds can barely comprehend how such a momentous event could occur so quietly. Yet the Gospels record no cheering crowds attending His arrival, no royal procession, no speeches, no reception worthy of a King. Surely this could not be the very Son of God! Why, there was no feast, no hubbub, no to-do, hardly any disturbance at all! Against all human logic, the Messiah slipped quietly into the world, virtually unannounced save to a lowly band of shepherds.

God often makes His really important moves in just this quiet way. In the Old Testament He illustrated this fact to the prophet Elijah. In 1 Kings 19:11–13, He revealed Himself not in the ways Elijah expected, not in the storm, not in the earthquake, nor in the raging fire, but in a still, small voice. He shows Himself to humanity the same way today. He doesn't produce huge, star-studded spectaculars to capture the world's attention. In fact, He most often seems to shun the world stage entirely.

Why does He choose to make Himself known in such a quiet, personal way? I think it is because God is more interested in each individual heart than in humanity as a whole. He doesn't so much love humanity as He loves each man, woman, and child. He doesn't so much want to intervene in human affairs as He does in the affairs of individuals. His design is that by changing individual lives, the world itself will be changed into a more loving, godly place. So He speaks quietly to each of us, in that still, small voice, hoping that we will hear His call and enter into the fellowship He offers.

This Christmas, will you allow Him to speak to your heart? Will you let Him begin changing the world by changing you? This is the real potential of His coming into the world. Christmas is not about lights, crowds, and presents—not really. The true meaning of Christmas is that He reveals Himself to each person who humbly seeks Him.

Take time this season to seek Him and His will for you. And expect to find Him. "Where meek souls will receive Him still, the dear Christ enters in."

- As your pace begins to quicken in these final days before Christmas, name some of the things that threaten to crowd out Christ.
- What can you do to slow things down in order to seek Christ, the real meaning of Christmas?
- Read Jeremiah 29:13. How important is it that you take the initiative to seek Him out?
- Begin now, even as the holiday pace escalates, to meditate before Him. Take in the peace that is found in His presence, and make your heart available to Him.

> *In the quietness of this moment, Lord, speak to my heart. I long to know You and feel Your presence with me. Take my heart and mold it to Your will. Begin Your healing work in the world by beginning in me. Amen.*

Of the Father's Love Begotten

Words: Aurelius Clemens Prudentius, 348–413
Tr. John Mason Neale, 1818–1866, and Henry W. Baker, 1821–1877

Music: 13th Century Plainsong Melody
Arr. Mark Blankenship, 1943–

Unison

1. Of the Fa - ther's love be - got - ten, Ere the worlds be - gan to be,
2. O ye heights of heav'n a - dore Him; An - gel hosts, His prais - es sing;
3. Christ, to Thee with God the Fa - ther, And, O Ho - ly Ghost, to Thee,

He is Al - pha and O - me - ga, He the source, the
Pow'rs, do - min - ions, bow be - fore Him, And ex - tol our
Hymn and chant and high thanks - giv - ing And un - wea - ried

end - ing He, Of the things that are, that have been,
God and King; Let no tongue on earth be si - lent,
prais - es be: Hon - or, glo - ry, and do - min - ion,

And that fu - ture years shall see, Ev - er - more and ev - er - more!
Ev - 'ry voice in con - cert ring, Ev - er - more and ev - er - more!
And e - ter - nal vic - to - ry, Ev - er - more and ev - er - more!

Of the Father's Love

For God so loved the world, that He gave His only begotten Son,
that whoever believes in Him should not perish, but have eternal life.

John 3:16

Christmas was different at our house last year. Breaking a tradition of relative-hopping, we finally spent Christmas day at home, alone. What a wonderful gift that was to ourselves. Instead of the regular "feeding frenzy" on brightly wrapped packages, my wife and I helped the children take time to savor every gift; they took all morning to open and play with each new toy. We all came away with a real appreciation of the bounteous blessings that had been waiting there for us under the tree. And we came away with a renewed appreciation for the givers of those gifts.

If you are a parent, you have no doubt had the experience of searching all over town for that one special toy your child just had to have. (I confess that via telephone my family actually searches from state to state.) No mere imitation would do, would it? It had to be the exact item, by the exact manufacturer, in the exact color! Having secured that treasure against all odds, do you remember your own excitement as you watched your child open that package? You knew in just a moment his eyes would light up, his face beaming with excitement. All would be right in his world because of that one special present, the one he just had to have.

I'll bet that is just how God felt when He gave us His one special gift, His Son. Like a loving parent, God has given us so many wonderful things. His blessings are poured out upon us daily in abundance. He obviously delights in our pleasure, so richly has He blessed us. But like a parent, He knows our minds sometimes better that we do ourselves. As the Creator of our hearts, He understands what it will take to make us genuinely happy. He knows that not even the daily gifts of sustenance will bring that lasting light to our eyes. In sending His Son to be our Savior, our heavenly Father gave a present that would place an eternal gleam in our eyes. Christ is the One special Gift that we just had to have; He makes everything right in our world. No substitute would do; we really had to have Him.

Take a moment of quality time with your heavenly Father. Thank Him for all of the blessings that are yours simply because He loves you. Thank Him for that deep, matchless love. And thank Him for that One special gift of His Son, the gift that makes all the others worthwhile.

- Beyond all the material things, what are the intangibles on your wish list this Christmas? What do you want for yourself on a deep, soul level? What do you want for the people you love?
- Ask the Giver of every good and perfect gift to grant you and the ones you love the fulfillment of all those unseen needs and wishes. And don't forget to thank Him for that most perfect gift, the gift of His Son.

Thank You, Father, for Your boundless love that saw my heart's need and reached out to meet it. Thank You for Your Son, who died that I might live, and Who lives that I might walk in the light of Your love. Amen.

In the Bleak Midwinter

Words: Christina G. Rossetti, 1830–1894

Music: Gustav Holst, 1874–1934

What Can I Give Him?

But God has chosen the foolish things of the world to shame the wise,
and. . .the weak things of the world to shame the things which are strong.

1 Corinthians 1:27

Not quite as popularly recognized as some Christmas carols, this one is the source of a better-known little verse that is at the same time childlike and profound.

> *What can I give Him, poor as I am?*
> *If I were a shepherd, I would bring a lamb;*
> *If I were a wise man, I would do my part;*
> *Yet what I can I give Him: give my heart.*

Sometimes we underestimate what God can do with the simplest of gifts. We peer anxiously into our storehouses of ability and find the shelves embarrassingly bare; we despair of ever having that something that is just right for His use. So discounting what we do have to offer, we meekly defer to others whom we deem wiser and stronger in the faith. But our thinking is exactly backward!

We are mistaken when we imagine that God requires some grand gift or talent from us. In fact, He is glorified far more by those offerings that are weaker and more unseemly. He doesn't want to compete with us for the glory, so He chooses to do His best work through those of us who appear to have the least to give.

Do you remember the story of the poor widow who gave all she had to God? Christ was pleased with her gift, while He scoffed at the rich men who made a show of their so-called sacrifices. He would rather use a thousand widows' mites than greater amounts given in pride. And, I really believe, He can bring more souls to salvation through a thousand ordinary people than through one famous evangelist.

Do you sometimes feel like a small fish in a very large pond? Do not despair; yours is the very life He desires to use to bring glory to Himself. Don't discount your usefulness to Him. After all, Jesus used a motley crew of fishermen, publicans, and zealots, the lowest strata of their society, to turn the world upside down. Today, He wants to use just such a collection of foolish weaklings as ourselves to confound the wise and mighty of our age.

- In the story of the Little Drummer Boy, a child realizes that he already possesses within himself the perfect gift for the Christ Child. What has God built into you that you can give back to Him? Do you have a talent or ability you can give Him? What about a personality trait, such as kindness? How about an attitude, like mercy or joy?
- Bring your gift to Him now. Present to Him the unique creation that is you, to use in whatever way He desires.

Heavenly Father, take my life and use it to bring honor to Yourself. Such simple talents as I have, I give to You. Remove from my heart the pride that would stifle Your Spirit. I humbly give You my best, in faith that it is the very thing that You desire. Amen.

Angels, from the Realms of Glory

Words: James Montgomery, 1771–1854

Music: Henry T. Smart, 1813–1879

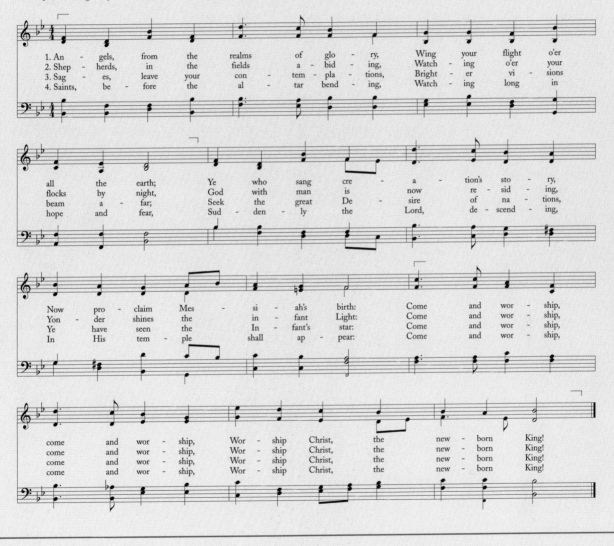

1. An - gels, from the realms of glo - ry, Wing your flight o'er
2. Shep - herds, in the fields a - bid - ing, Watch - ing o'er your
3. Sag - es, leave your con - tem - pla - tions, Bright - er vi - sions
4. Saints, be - fore the al - tar bend - ing, Watch - ing long in

all the earth; Ye who sang cre - a - tion's sto - ry,
flocks by night, God with man is now re - sid - ing,
beam a - far; Seek the great De - sire of na - tions,
hope and fear, Sud - den - ly the Lord, de - scend - ing,

Now pro - claim Mes - si - ah's birth: Come and wor - ship,
Yon - der shines the in - fant Light: Come and wor - ship,
Ye have seen the In - fant's star: Come and wor - ship,
In His tem - ple shall ap - pear: Come and wor - ship,

come and wor - ship, Wor - ship Christ, the new - born King!
come and wor - ship, Wor - ship Christ, the new - born King!
come and wor - ship, Wor - ship Christ, the new - born King!
come and wor - ship, Wor - ship Christ, the new - born King!

The Infant Light

He was in the beginning with God.

John 1:2

"Ye who sang creation's story, now proclaim Messiah's birth." The angels of highest heaven had assembled that night to proclaim good tidings of great joy and exalt God. This was no new experience for the heavenly host, for they were created for this very purpose. They had been present when the world and all that is in it came into being. At the beginning of time as we know it, these heavenly creatures had lifted their voices in anthems of praise to the Creator. Now that same multitude had gathered to witness and proclaim a second amazing act of love: the redemption of the human race.

Sometimes all the nativity crèches and pageants, with their depictions of Baby Jesus, lull us into forgetting that Bethlehem's Newborn was not really all that new. John tells us that He was in the beginning with God. He was the very image of God, and He had existed from eternity (John 1:1–3). The only thing new about Him that night was His form, for He entered into our history taking upon Himself the body of a human baby.

The second stanza of the carol "Angels from the Realms of Glory" uses a wonderfully appropriate phrase to describe the paradox of God the Creator existing in the form of a human creature: "Yonder shines the infant Light." The infant Light; this Baby was the Light that, according to John's Gospel, "coming into the world, enlightens every man" (John 1:9). He was the very essence and embodiment of eternal truth, and yet He had all the vulnerabilities and limitations of a human baby. Imagine the Omnipotent One, a Baby; the Almighty, a helpless Child!

Try as we might, we will never quite understand how these opposite realities can coexist.

Nevertheless, we need to remember and take to heart that He was no ordinary child. He did not come, as some claim, to be a good teacher or even a great prophet. This Baby, though fully human, was unique among humankind. In some wondrous way, He was God, the eternal One superimposed onto the time line of human events. He came into the world to be a Light in our darkness, to save us from a state of separation from God.

This same Light stands ready to enlighten your heart and banish the personal darkness of sin in your life. In your mind, see Him outgrowing the cradle, becoming mature, dying for you on the cross, and rising in triumph over sin. See Him as He really is, reigning victoriously at the right hand of God. Don't leave Him in the manger, for He is oh so much more than just another baby!

- In what ways is Christ a Light to humanity? In what ways is He a Light to you personally?
- Are there areas of darkness in your life that need to feel the rays of His light? What are they?
- What can you do throughout the coming year to let the eternal Light who is Christ shine continually in and through your life?

Christ Jesus, I recognize You as more than a holy Baby. You are the Lord of Glory and the Light of the World. Cast Your brilliant rays upon me and light my world. Amen.

Good Christian Men, Rejoice

Words: Medieval Latin Carol, 14th Century
Tr. John Mason Neale, 1818–1866

Music: Traditional German Carol, 14th Century

1. Good Chris - tian men, re - joice With heart and soul and voice!
2. Good Chris - tian men, re - joice With heart and soul and voice!
3. Good Chris - tian men, re - joice With heart and soul and voice!

Give ye heed to what we say: Je - sus Christ is born to - day.
Now ye hear of end - less bliss: Je - sus Christ was born for this.
Now ye need not fear the grave: Je - sus Christ was born to save;

Man and beast be - fore Him bow, And He is in the man - ger now:
He has o - pened heav - en's door, And man is blest for - ev - er - more.
Calls you one and calls you all, To gain His ev - er - last - ing hall.

Christ is born to - day, Christ is born to - day!
Christ was born for this, Christ was born for this!
Christ was born to save, Christ was born to save!

With Heart and Soul and Voice

Rejoice in the Lord always; again I will say, rejoice!

Philippians 4:4

"'Tis the season to be jolly, fa la la la la. . ." Christmas is supposed to be a joyous time of cheerful thoughts and warm feelings. Yet statisticians tell us that depression is at its highest level nationwide during the holiday season. Some of us simply have nothing to be cheerful about. For others Christmas brings painful thoughts of loved ones departed. For others still, the family orientation of the holiday is a sad reminder of love never received, needs never met. From what reserves can these souls draw the extra measure of joy this season seems to require of them? How can they "rejoice" when there is nothing to smile about?

Believe it or not, it is possible to rejoice without necessarily being happy. That's because, while happiness is linked to favorable circumstances, rejoicing springs from a trust in God that transcends the daily events of our lives. In exhorting us to rejoice, the Bible is not so much issuing a command to be happy all the time as it is revealing to us a wonderful possibility: There is an alternative to despair. In Christ we can know a kind of joy that weathers even our deepest sorrow.

In his letter to the Philippian Christians, Paul the apostle encourages his readers to rejoice, concluding with this exhortation: "Be anxious for nothing, but in everything. . .let your requests be made known to God. And the peace of God, which surpasses all comprehension, shall guard your hearts and your minds in Christ Jesus" (Philippians 4:6–7). Paul faced many trials because of his faith; and yet he was able to write, "I have learned to be content in whatever circumstance I am" (Philippians 4:11). He spoke of a quiet, battle-hardened confidence in Christ that freed him, even while shackled in jail, to sing hymns of praise until the walls literally shook! I believe Paul understood two keys to rejoicing.

First, Paul understood that God does not necessarily design our lives to make us happy. God is much more concerned with strengthening our character—a sometimes painful process. But if we have made God our Lord, we can be confident that He will use even the crises in our lives to mature us into Christ's likeness. We don't have to be life's aimless victims. Though harsh things may happen to us, God is still fully able to work in us.

Second, Paul understood that while happiness is an emotion over which we may have little control, rejoicing is an action, a choice. Unlike happiness, it is not a state of being but a state of doing. In choosing to rejoice we choose to reaffirm our trust that God is greater than any situation in which we may find ourselves. Rejoicing is the vehicle by which we choose to lean on God for strength, rather than depending on our own, sometimes meager, emotional resources.

The first step toward joy is to surrender your past, present, and future to Christ. As His Lordship takes hold, you will find that He is more than sufficient to handle the trials in your life.

- We all have things in our lives that bring unhappiness. What are some of the things that rob you of joy, peace, or security?
- Regardless of your feelings about these things, do you think they are really beyond God's control?
- Can you choose to let go of these matters and lay them before God? By choosing to rejoice, can you affirm your trust in the way He will handle your life?

Lord Jesus, take my anxieties and fears. Replace them with inner joy that comes from the assurance that You are greater than the difficulties I face. Amen.

The Holly and the Ivy

Words: Traditional English Carol

Music: Traditional English Melody
Harm. Thomas L. Pless, 1960–

To Be Our Sweet Savior

For this I have been born, and for this I have come into the world.
John 18:37

In Britain, the use of holly dates back to the time of pagan festivals. But by the time this folk carol was recorded, holly had come to be thought of as a symbol of Christ's suffering death on the cross. The white blossom was seen as an emblem of His holiness and purity; the bright red berry represented His shed blood. The prickly leaves brought to mind the crown of thorns He was made to wear, while the bitterness of the bark recalled the cup of gall He was given to drink.

So while it is light enough at first hearing, this simple little carol actually puts us in mind of the bleaker side of Christ's purpose here on earth. Why, in a season of rejoicing and lights, should we be brought to ponder this heavier, darker aspect of our faith? This carol seems to be wholly out of place at such a joyful time of year. Why must we mar the holiday celebration with a song more suited to Holy Week, that period between Palm Sunday and Easter, when we traditionally meditate on Christ's suffering and death?

Very simply, the appearance of this carol at Christmastime serves as a reminder that apart from His atoning death, Christ's birth would have had little meaning. Anyone can be born. It happens thousands of times every day. As much a miracle as it seems to mommies and daddies at that blessed moment, childbirth has occurred billions upon billions of times all around the world throughout history. So there was nothing inherently special about the birth of another Jewish baby in Bethlehem. But there was something very significant about what this Baby was born to do. As miraculous as it was that God would come to dwell among us, that was not all the angels were celebrating that night as they sang before the shepherds. What would happen as a result of His being here is what moved the heavens to song. Viewed against the backdrop of His sacrificial death and victorious resurrection, we understand that the nativity was important not for what it meant that night, but for what it would eventually mean to all humankind. This Baby was born into the world to bring the gift of salvation and eternal life to those whom God loved so much.

We would do well to reserve some time at Christmas to think about the enormous sacrifice in which our holiday joy is rooted. We must not take this magnificent gift for granted. We are free to live each day in the light of God's love—because the little Lamb of God who was born that night grew up to die for our debt of sin. This is the real significance of Christmas.

- In your own words, why was Jesus born into the world? What was God's ultimate goal in sending His Son?
- Read John 3:16. What do you suppose was God's motivation for sending His Son to save us from sin?
- Realizing what the Christ Child was born to do, should Christmas be a joyful time, a somber time, or both? Why?
- Can you think of a worthy response to God's great love and sacrifice? How can we thank Him?

Lord, I am humbled when I consider the depth of love You showed me on the cross. I offer You my praise as a partial payment of the debt of love I owe. May I be worthy of the great price You paid for me. Amen.

O Come, All Ye Faithful

Words: Latin hymn; ascribed to John Francis Wade, c. 1711–1786
Tr. Frederick Oakeley, 1802–1880 and others

Music: John Francis Wade, c.1711–1786

1. O come, all ye faithful, joyful and tri - um - phant, O come ye, O come ye to Beth - le - hem! Come and be - hold Him, born the King of an - gels! O come, let us a - dore Him, O come, let us a - dore Him, O come, let us a - dore Him, Christ the Lord!

2. Sing, choirs of an - gels, sing in ex - ul - ta - tion, O sing, all ye bright hosts of heav'n a - bove! Glo - ry to God, all glo - ry in the high - est!

3. Yea, Lord, we greet Thee, born this hap - py morn - ing, Je - sus, to Thee be all glo - ry giv'n; Word of the Fa - ther, now in flesh ap - pear - ing!

Let Us Adore Him!

Let everything that has breath praise the LORD.

Psalm 150:6

"Sing, choirs of angels, sing in exultation! . . . Jesus, to Thee be all glory giv'n! . . . O come, let us adore Him, Christ the Lord!" "O Come, All Ye Faithful" has much in common with the 150th Psalm. Like that Scripture passage, it stirs us to concentrate our souls' best energies on glorifying the Lord. It reminds us that praise is the proper response when we enter into the presence of God.

Christ is inherently worthy of our worship. Not just for what He has done, though He has certainly blessed us richly; He deserves our worship because of who He is. Not that He, in His omnipotence, demands our praise, like a self-centered child. No, it is simply intrinsic to His nature that He should be at the center of our attention, as it is intrinsic to our original nature that we should praise Him. For this we have been created. Revelation 4:11 tells us that we exist, as the King James Version aptly puts it, "for thy pleasure." When we worship Him and give Him priority in our lives, we are simply operating according to design.

Our universe exists, we know, according to certain governing principles; our knowledge of these is largely limited to the fields of science and mathematics. Beyond these narrow confines, however, is a purposeful universal order that reaches past natural physical laws to include a dynamic spiritual dimension. We can only understand a fraction of this, but this much we do know: We are at our best when we live in submission to our Creator. Allowing Him His proper place in our lives naturally stimulates all that is noble and good within our souls. But when we give in to the selfishness that hides in the heart of each one of us, our lives and ultimately our world are soon out of balance. When we choose to dwell upon the throne rather than before it, we disturb the order of creation. Evil, desperation, and despair are the result.

The world is in need of men and women who know how to praise God, for we as a people have wandered far from His throne room. Peace, hope, and love are in short supply, even at Christmastime. These qualities are not, you see, just natural outgrowths of the holidays. Instead, they flow from hearts that are in right relationship to heaven. If peace and love are to flourish in the world, it will be because you and I choose to focus our attention on the Lord.

Worship the Lord right now. You may want to use as a guide Revelation 5:11–14, a passage that depicts the quality of praise that God is accustomed to receiving. As you worship, don't just recognize His dominion over the earth. Give Him dominion over your heart as well, for this is true worship.

- What is the difference between having God as a part of your life and having Him as the center of your life?
- Read Revelation 5:12. What does it mean to give Christ power, riches, and strength? Doesn't He

already possess these things in abundance? Whose power, riches, and strength can you give Him?

• What strengths do you have? What power? What riches? Are you willing to give these to Him for His pleasure? This is true worship.

Holy God, I enter into Your presence not with mere words of praise, but with genuine humility, recognizing that You are worthy to reign on the throne of my life. Plant in me a desire to live and flourish in Your presence. Amen.

CHRISTMAS DAY

CELEBRATION

The King of Glory

"   ift up your heads, O gates,

And lift them up, O ancient doors,

That the King of glory may come in!

Who is this King of glory?

The LORD of hosts,

He is the King of glory."

Psalm 24:9–10

Joy to the World!

Words: Isaac Watts, 1674–1748

Music: George Frederick Handel, 1685–1759
Arr. Lowell Mason, 1792–1872

Let Earth Receive Her King

I bring you good tidings of great joy, which shall be to all people.
Luke 2:10

Christmas is here! That holiest of holidays has finally arrived, with all the sights, sounds, scents, and sensations that say this is a day unlike any other of the year. This is the birthday of the King!

Christmas is here, and we can hear the song of the angels echoing through the corridors of time: "O come, all ye faithful, come to Bethlehem; come, let us adore Him, Christ the Lord!" Customs have changed from century to century and from place to place, but ever since that long-ago night when the angelic host appeared to the shepherds, a continual chorus of praise has flowed as one generation after another has responded to the call, "Come and worship; worship Christ the newborn King." Today that call to celebrate falls on our ears. It is our turn to kneel before Him and take up the song. How shall we approach the manger that has become a throne? What gift shall we bring? What can we do to ensure that our offering is worthy of the Holy Baby?

Because the Christ of Christmas bridged the gap between heaven and Earth, we are blessed to live in an age of grace. So worship for us is not as much a matter of form as it is a state of the heart. We have been set free to enjoy the benefits of Christ's claim that, "an hour is coming, and now is, when the true worshipers shall worship the Father in spirit and truth" (John 4:23). Indeed, He continues, "for such people the Father seeks to be His worshipers."

As we consider what would be a suitable birthday gift for the King, shouldn't we give to Him the very thing He seeks? In His eyes, there is no greater gift than a soul bowed before Him in honesty and humility, and there is no substitute for a pure heart. He does not value pomp and splendor; high praise is a commodity in heaven, and surely we could never compete with the seraphim! What, then, does He desire? A heart that welcomes Him to make His home there. If you want to give to Him, you must receive Him. No short-term, onetime gift will suffice; He wishes to dwell in each of our hearts for the rest of our lives. This is what He desires most. No other offering could ever be worthy of His great sacrifice.

On this busy day, bow your head before Him for one quiet moment. Still your soul, emptying it of anything that might keep you from entertaining your heavenly Guest. Now, very literally, receive your King; willingly ask Him to be at home within you. Commit to Him, or recommit, every aspect of your daily life. Surrender your longings and desires to Him. Let Him know that as much as you are able, you are ready to follow in whatever direction He may lead. Submit yourself to His Lordship, for no other gift will do. Nothing less than your entire self is enough, not when He loved you so much that He came into the world to be your Savior.

- Christmas is not ultimately about children. It is not about feelings of peace and love. It is not about family. It is about receiving Christ as King of our lives. Are you prepared to offer to Him the gift that He most desires, your very heart and soul?
- Bow before Him and lift up to Christ the only gift you have that is worthy of this great occasion—His right to rule as King in your life.

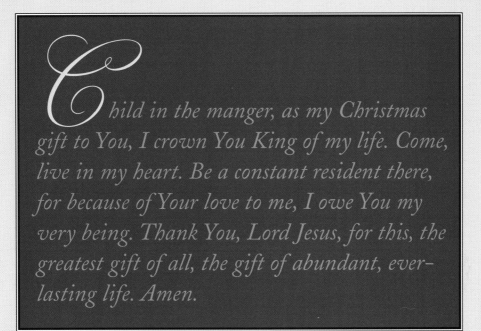

Child in the manger, as my Christmas gift to You, I crown You King of my life. Come, live in my heart. Be a constant resident there, for because of Your love to me, I owe You my very being. Thank You, Lord Jesus, for this, the greatest gift of all, the gift of abundant, everlasting life. Amen.

About the Author

Thomas L. Pless is an ordained Southern Baptist minister with a passion for Christian worship and discipleship. He holds a Master of Music degree from Southwestern Baptist Theological Seminary. In addition to a widely varied teaching ministry, he is a composer of choral and contemporary gospel music. He is currently the director of Promise Ministries, a contemporary vocal ensemble featured in concert. Charlotte, North Carolina is home to Reverend Pless, his wife, and their two children.